4.95
it Event

Slavery Today

Kaye Stearman

RSVP
RAINTREE
STECK-VAUGHN
PUBLISHERS
A Steck-Vaughn Company

Austin, Texas

Talking Points series
Alcohol
Animal Rights
Charities—Do They Work?
Divorce
Genocide
Homelessness
Mental Illness
Slavery Today

Published by Raintree Steck-Vaughn Publishers,
an imprint of Steck-Vaughn Company

Library of Congress Cataloging-in-Publication Data
Stearman, Kaye.
Slavery today / Kaye Stearman.
        p.   cm.—(Talking points)
        Includes bibliographical references and index.
        Summary: Explains the nature of slavery and
        examines the existence of forced labor today,
        discussing such areas as child workers, migrant
        workers, and trafficking in people.
        ISBN 0-8172-5320-3
        1. Slavery—Juvenile literature.
        [1. Slavery. 2. Forced labor.]
        I. Title. II. Series: Talking points.
        HT871.S74 1999
        306.3'62—dc21   98-33205

Printed in Italy. Bound in the United States.
1 2 3 4 5 6 7 8 9 0 04 03 02 01 00

Picture acknowledgments:
Ronald Sheridan's Ancient Art and
Architecture Collection 3; Anti-Slavery
International 9 (Drik/APN & Shioshab), 20–21
(Ben Buxton), 26, 45; Camera Press Ltd *cover*
(B. Gysembergh), 8–9; Sue Cunningham
Photographic 11; The International Labour
Office 15 (J. Maillard), 17, 22 (Philippe
Lissac), 24 (P. Lissac), 30 (J. Maillard), 33 (M.
Trajtenberg), 36 (P. Lissac), 58 (J. Maillard);
Impact Photos Ltd. 41 (Alain le Garsmeur);
Panos Pictures 5 (Sean Sprague), 14 (S.
Sprague), 20, 25 (Paul Smith), 34 (Chris
Stower), 37 (Anders Gunnart), 39 (Stephen
Gill), 40 (S. Sprague), 44 (Penny Tweedie), 50
(Nic Dunlop), 56 (S. Sprague), 57 (Howard
Davies); Library of Congress 10; Popperfoto 4,
7, 28, 31, 35, 38, 42 (Winston Sng), 43
(Patrick de Noirmont), 47 (Simone Kreitem),
48 (Apichart Weerawong), 49, 53 (Paul
Barker), 55 (David Ahmed); Still Pictures 12
(Jorgen Schytle), 13 (J. Schytle), 16 (Shehzad
Noorani), 18 (Gil Moti), 19 (Mark Edwards),
21 (Christian Aid: M. Cottingham), 27 (Paul
Harrison), 32 (Gill Moti), 45 (Mark Edwards),
54 (Hartmut Schwarzbach); Tony Stone Images
51 (Glen Allison), 59 (Thia Konig), Topham
Picturepoint 23 (Kelvoord/The Image Works),
29 (Marquez), 52.

The author would like to thank Victoria
Richardson for help with translations.

Contents

Thinking about slavery

A slave is a person who is wholly or partly owned by another person or organization. Slaves have no rights over their own bodies. Their time and labor are not their own. The work they do and the hours they work are decided by others, and the rewards from their work belong to others. Slaves are not free to decide whom they work for or where they live.

The horrors of slavery have been documented through the ages, including the twentieth century.

Although slavery has taken many forms, slaves are nearly always the groups with the fewest rights and lowest status in society. Slavery has existed in different societies throughout history. However, it is wrong to think that slavery exists only in the pages of history books. Today, slavery is no longer considered lawful or publicly acceptable. Yet millions of people in many countries continue to live in slavery, often hidden from the world.

Small children pick coffee in Guatemala. The work is hard for adults as well as children.

To begin to consider what slavery means and how it might affect people's lives, the following case studies introduce us to five different people—all slaves—who were or are victims of just a few of the many different forms of slavery.

Case studies: Forms of slavery

Bassus's story

News has come through of the slave uprisings in Rome. Bassus admires the courage of the rebels, but he knows that they have no chance of winning. He dreams that one day his master will free him.

Southern Italy, A.D. 71

Nana's story

Nana still has nightmares about how he was caught and sold to the white men. He remembers those who died on the terrible ocean voyage. Now he must survive the endless backbreaking labor of the tobacco plantation.

North America, 1700

Leonid's story

Once, Leonid had been a trusted member of the Communist party, with a bright future. Then, he was declared an "enemy of the people," put on trial, and sent to a labor camp in the Arctic. Now he lives in fear.

Kola Peninsula, northern Russia, 1936

Carla's story

Picking coffee beans is hard work, especially for a seven-year-old. But Carla has no choice—she must work to survive. The wages are low, and conditions are terrible. But it is the only work available.

Coastal plain of Guatemala, 1979

Sheela's story

Sheela works every waking hour—washing, cleaning, baby-sitting, serving food. She is only 12 years old. Sheela is very lonely, because her family lives far away. But, normally, she is so tired she cannot even cry herself to sleep.

Nagpur, India, 1998

Labor without reward

So what does it really mean when we say that a slave's time and labor are not his or her own? If we look in more detail at the lives of three of the slaves to whom we were introduced on the previous pages —Bassus from ancient Rome, Nana in North America, and Leonid from the former Soviet Union—we will see how slaves can be forced to work for others without receiving any reward or having any say in how, where, or when they work.

Bassus and Nana lived in societies where slavery was lawful. In Roman times the legal term for a slave was an *instrumentum vocale*, literally a speaking tool. At the time of the Atlantic slave trade, when millions of Africans were sold in the Americas and the Caribbean to work as slave laborers, slaves were regarded as "cargo," not people. In both societies, slaves could be bought and sold by their owners. This is known as chattel slavery. Sometimes slaves were given their freedom by their owners or bought their own freedom.

The Roman Empire needed slaves to work the farms of the wealthy citizens or to build public monuments. Nearly 1,000 years later, in the former Soviet Union, prisoners built roads, railroads, dams, and factories. They also logged timber and mined coal across the vast, harsh landscape.

Slave labor supported the luxurious lifestyles of rich people in ancient Rome.

Soviet prisoners, called *zeks*, were housed in labor camps, surrounded by watchtowers. Some *zeks* were criminals, but many, like Leonid, were political prisoners.

For a 10-hour working day, Leonid received a basic ration: bread, soup, and *kasha* (gruel). Like Bassus and Nana, he was not paid wages. Unlike Bassus and Nana, he could never buy his freedom. He could only hope to be released at the end of his long sentence. It is estimated that in 1938 there were 8 million *zeks*. It is thought that each year about 10 percent of them died from the effects of starvation and exhaustion.

In the former Soviet Union, political prisoners labored in vast camps in remote areas.

Talking point

"No one shall be held in slavery or servitude; slavery and the slave trade shall be prohibited in all their forms."

Article 4 of the United Nations' Universal Declaration of Human Rights

If everyone knows slavery is wrong, why do you think it is necessary for human rights documents to ban slavery and the slave trade?

Slaves to the system

Carla and Sheela, whom we met on page 5, are not owned by their masters or imprisoned by their government. They work for wages—Carla for a big company and Sheela for a family. They are slaves because their time and labor belong to others.

Coffee picking

Carla and her family are Maya Indians from the highlands of Guatemala. In 1979, their farm was too small to support the family. So, in the following years, they migrated to the coastal plains to harvest the coffee and sugarcane on the large commercial farms. Wages were very low, and some workers were paid in food, not with money. Hours were long, and working conditions were very bad. Many of the coffee pickers were very young children.

Carla and her family have become enslaved by their poverty. They have to work to live and have little choice about what work they do. Little has changed for Carla and her family, and others like them, since 1979.

In many countries poverty pushes young girls into domestic service, leaving them isolated and exploited.

Slaves in Uganda

In northern Uganda, young people are regularly kidnapped by rebels known as the Lord's Resistance Army. The children are given military training and forced to become killers. Sometimes they must kill family members. The girls are ordered to "marry" the rebel soldiers. In the three years between 1995 and 1998 more than 8,000 young people were enslaved in this way.

Payday—but many child domestic servants never see their wages

Child servant

At least Carla remains with her family. Sheela has no friends or family to turn to and no outside life or contacts. Although the family she works for has children her age, she is expected to act as their servant and obey their every order. She sleeps on a mat in a corner of the kitchen. Her parents received her first month's wages from her employer, but there have been no further payments.

Carla and Sheela are slaves because they have been sent to work for another family or organization, without the right to refuse. They have no control over their wages or conditions. Often these conditions are dangerous or hazardous. Poverty and lack of opportunities have pushed both girls into slavery. Neither knows of any rights they might possess, especially since neither can read or write. They are particularly vulnerable because as young people, they are smaller, weaker, and less powerful than their employers.

It may be hard to believe that slavery still occurs as we enter the twenty-first century, but the evidence speaks for itself: slavery still exists today. This book looks at modern forms of slavery, how and where they exist, and how slavery affects the lives of millions of people worldwide. It also looks at campaigns against slavery and at what ordinary people, like ourselves, can do to help end slavery.

The ties that bind

The Atlantic slave trade, which continued for 400 years, was based on capturing, trafficking in, and selling people for profit. Africans were captured by other Africans or Europeans and sold to European slave traders. In turn, slave traders shipped their captives to the Americas where they were sold to the European owners of the sugar, cotton, and tobacco plantations.

The Atlantic slave trade was highly organized, lawful, and openly conducted. It made slavers and plantation owners wealthy and helped finance Europe's Industrial Revolution. It was also a very cruel trade causing terrible loss of human life. Slaves were not regarded as humans, and their lives were valued only in terms of profit and loss. More than 10 million Africans became chattel slaves. Huge numbers died on the voyage or on the plantations of ill-treatment, disease, or overwork. Some slaves escaped. A few bought, or were given, their freedom.

Campaigning for freedom

The Atlantic slave trade finally ceased for several complex reasons. One important reason was that a few people in Europe and America, including former slaves, campaigned against slavery. Gradually, countries passed laws, first against slave trading and then against slave owning. Most laws were passed in the nineteenth century, but the fight against slavery continued well into the twentieth century. After 1919 the new League of Nations became the main forum for antislavery campaigns, a role later taken over by its successor, the United Nations.

These two American slave children, Isaac and Rosa, were photographed in 1863 after being given their freedom.

The story goes on

Slavery in Africa continued after the end of the Atlantic slave trade. Along the East African coast, Arab slave traders sold Africans to Asia and the Middle East. Then, in the twentieth century, authorities in many African countries tried to end slavery. However, in more remote areas it was hard to control, and slavery continued—especially in and around the Sahara desert. Now, at the end of the twentieth century, although most slavery has disappeared, in a few areas a shocking number of people still are enslaved.

Talking point

"Beyond doubt it was the slave trade which raised Liverpool from a struggling port to one of the most richest [sic] and prosperous trading centers in the world."

Ramsey Muir, historian and politician, United Kingdom, 1907

Do you think that history books always give the full story about slavery? What do you know about slavery in your country's history?

The dateline below gives the most important dates in the fight against slavery.

Dateline

1802 Denmark bans trading in slaves
1807 Great Britain bans the slave trade in British colonies
1809 The U.S. bans its citizens from international slave trade
1820 Spain bans slave trade in Spanish colonies
      (except Cuba)
1833 Great Britain frees slaves in British colonies
1848 France bans slavery and frees slaves in
      French colonies
1853 Brazil bans slave trade
1863 President Lincoln frees slaves in the U.S. on January 1
1886 Cuba bans slavery
1888 Brazil frees slaves
1962 Saudi Arabia bans slavery
1976 India bans bonded labor
1980 Mauritania bans slavery
1992 Pakistan bans bonded labor

The Freedom Statue in Zambia, Southern Africa, shows a slave breaking his chains.

11

Slavery in Mauritania

One region where slavery continues to exist is Mauritania, the vast desert country in the north-west corner of Africa. Once, most Mauritanians lived a nomadic life in the desert, but today most have settled in the towns to escape the bonds of slavery. Life in Nouakchott, the capital, is hard and insecure. There are few jobs, housing is poor, and there is the constant fear of discovery. But many people prefer insecurity to life as a slave.

Slavery has existed in Mauritania for centuries. Traditionally, some groups and tribes were slave masters while others were born into slavery. Some slaves lived in their master's household, others farmed the master's lands but lived separately. Many slaves were not actually sold but were transferred between slave-owning families, sometimes as exchanges or "gifts."

In 1980 the Mauritanian government declared that slavery was to end. In 1981 a new law said that all slaves were to be freed and become full citizens, and that slave owners would be given money to make up for their loss. The law was not publicized and made little impact. Most slaves lived in remote areas and knew nothing of the law. There were no plans or programs to help slaves to become free citizens, no money to compensate slave owners, and no punishments for those who continued to hold slaves. As a result the law helped very few people.

Anti-Slavery International believes that there may be 100,000 slaves and 300,000 former slaves (over 1 in 6 of the population of 2.2 million), and called for further research into slavery in Mauritania.

Street life in Nouakchott, the capital of Mauritania. The city provides a haven for many runaway slaves.

Case study: Madame Aichana's story

Escape is difficult, but it is better than waiting for government action. In the Mauritanian city of Nouakchott there are many former slaves, some of whom are educated and can provide help and support. Escape is easier for men than for women and children.

One woman who escaped was Aichana Mint Boilil. Born into slavery, she had worked for her master, Mohammed Ould Moissa, since childhood. She was 13 when her master gave her to his cousin to repay a debt. Years later she was returned to Mohammed Ould Moissa who shared her services with several other relatives.

During these years Madame Aichana gave birth to five children; the fathers of the children were her masters, who also owned the children. When Madame Aichana finally escaped to Nouakchott, her children were seized by Mohammed Ould Moissa. They were returned much later, after support by antislavery campaigners inside and outside Mauritania.

The ties of children and family make it especially difficult for women to escape slavery.

Beliefs about slavery

The ties that bind a slave to his or her master are often much more than ties of property. They are also personal and family ties. Masters and slaves can share the same household. They can live, work, and travel together. Masters usually believe that they are superior people and that it is right and proper for slaves to serve them. In addition, many slaves believe that they should accept their position in life without complaint, even feeling that it is their religious duty to be a slave.

To justify why slavery exists in their society, some religious leaders quote the saying: "For a slave the way to heaven is under your master's foot." The ties of slavery are such that it is quite common to find that, long after they have gained their freedom, some former slaves make a money payment to their master's families.

SOS Esclaves

Breaking the ties of slavery is difficult, especially in poor countries like Mauritania and Sudan, where there is no public welfare system.

Slavery in Sudan

Africa's largest country, Sudan has, like Mauritania, had a long history of slave trading. Some time around 1985 new reports of slavery began to emerge, mainly in areas where the government supplied weapons to local armies to use against rebels. These local armies raided areas farther south and returned with captives, mainly women and children, who were forced to work in the soldiers' households and given or sold to friends or supporters. The government does little to stop the raids or help restore captives to their families.

Local armies in Sudan have captured women and children and sold them into slavery.

Governments often deny that slavery exists, and they are not interested in reforms such as giving land to former slaves to allow them to live independently. In Mauritania, it was not until 1997 that slavery could be discussed in the media. Despite obstacles, local groups have campaigned against slavery. These groups include SOS Esclaves (SOS Slaves), an organization of former slaves. In 1998, four SOS Esclaves members were imprisoned for taking part in a French television documentary about Mauritania. As long as slavery remains a hidden subject, escape to the city will remain the only way out for slaves.

Breaking the ties of slavery and forced labor is especially difficult in poor countries.

Debt bondage

Debt bondage is common in South Asia (India, Pakistan, Nepal), where it is known as bonded labor, and in some South American countries, especially Brazil. Debt bondage involves families and individuals.

The United Nations

The United Nations 1956 Convention on Slavery states that debt bondage is a form of slavery. It says that debt bondage occurs where a borrower (debtor) agrees to work for a lender to pay off a debt. What actually happens is that the work is given very low value, or the work conditions and repayment of the debt are not made clear. As a result, the debtor never pays off the debt and so must continue working for the lender.

Talking point

"What is wrong with the system? We have land and we need laborers to plow the fields. We lend them money and food and in return they work for us. Yes, sometimes they work hard but they do not starve and they have somewhere to live. If I give them money, they will spend it on alcohol."

Landlord from Nepal

Do you agree with this landlord? If you do, what are your reasons? If you do not, what is it about this statement that you think is wrong?

A young boy working in a cigarette factory in Bangladesh. His tiny wages are paid directly to his mother.

The poorest people may have to work into old age to pay off family debts taken on years before.

Unwritten laws

It is not the debt itself that is the problem, but the repayment. After all, many people borrow money to buy a house or car and then repay the debt over time. This is acceptable when everyone understands the terms of the agreement. Most countries have laws on lending and borrowing to protect both the debtor and the lender.

Debt bondage is very different. Here, one person borrows money or goods from another and in return agrees to work to repay the debt and the interest. The details of the loan are not clear, and there is no written contract. The debtor does not know how much he or she has paid off, the rate of interest, or the repayment period. But, why do people enter into such unfair contracts?

Debt bondage flourishes in countries where very poor people do not have enough land to support themselves and cannot earn a living. Their only asset is their ability to work. Some work for wages, but very often they have to borrow to survive. Generally, the lender is a landlord or local businessman. The debtor may work for years to repay the loan. Many never manage to repay the lender. They live and die in debt and pass the debt on to their children.

17

Case study: Ram's story

Debt bondage can work in many different ways. One example among millions is Ram Paswan. Although he is in his twenties, years of constant hard work in the fields make him look much older. Ram's family lives in the plains of eastern Nepal. They have always been poor, but over the years life has become much harder because land has risen in value, increasing the power of the big landowners.

Once, Ram's family worked for wages. They could manage from day to day, but whenever there was a big expense, such as medical treatment or a daughter's dowry, they had to borrow from the landlord—sometimes money and sometimes food. Now, they are completely dependent. They live in a tiny hut on the landlord's land. In return the whole family provides free labor for the landlord's fields.

Bonded laborers provide free labor for the landlords' fields. Even small children must work to repay debts.

Although Ram remembers the amount he borrowed, he does not understand how interest is calculated or how his labor is valued. He knows he is being cheated, but he cannot prove it. There is no written contract, but in any case he cannot read or write. He cannot borrow from a bank because there is none nearby, and if there were, it would not lend to him because he cannot offer security. He cannot protest because the landlord would beat him and remove the family from their home.

Ram dreams of leaving Nepal and finding work in India, perhaps as a servant or watchman. That way he could pay off the family debts and maybe even buy some land of his own. But the chances are that in India he would also find himself in debt, to a new employer or to a moneylender. Back in the village his family would continue to depend on the landlord.

In many countries in Asia tradition is very important and becomes another excuse to exploit the poor. In Nepal, most landowners belong to high castes, while laborers like Ram are low caste. Traditionally, high castes have high status in society and will not do heavy work. For them, keeping low-caste families in debt insures they will always have people to do the heavy work, like plowing, digging ditches, tending animals, and carrying water—and it is much cheaper than paying normal wages. The cheapest way for landowners to continue making a profit is if the debts of their bonded laborers are never paid off and are passed from one generation to another, providing free labor for decades.

The gap between the well-off landlord and the landless laborer is huge.

Factory bondage

Most debt bondage is in agriculture, but it also occurs in other areas, such as industry. Often it involves children. A parent takes an advance payment from a factory owner or an agent and, in return, bonds a child to work for them until the debt is repaid. In these cases, the child is a slave twice over—as a bonded laborer and as a child laborer.

Many children used as bonded laborers work in brick kilns, carrying heavy loads in hazardous conditions.

Children are often bonded to work in dangerous or hazardous industries. In southern Asia children work in brick kilns and stone quarries, in carpet and glassmaking, in match and firework factories, in making *bidis* (Indian cigarettes), and in polishing diamonds. Most are expected to work 12 or more hours a day. They damage their health, sometimes losing limbs or eyesight, or even their lives—all to pay a debt.

India's Abolition of Bonded Labor law of 1976 proclaims that bonded laborers should be freed from their debts and be rehabilitated into society. However, this has proven very difficult, because poverty and landlessness force poor people into debt. Most laborers and landlords do not know of the law or how it is supposed to work. Only when local campaigners get involved have bonded laborers been released. Pakistan passed a law in 1992 that has yet to make any real impact, and Nepal has no laws at all against bonded labor.

Working for change

The Bonded Labor Liberation Front (BLLF) of India was founded in 1981 by Swami Agnivesh, a human rights campaigner. He was horrified to find bonded laborers working in brick kilns and quarries near Delhi, India's capital city, although bonded labor was banned by law in 1976. Local BLLF activists identify groups of bonded laborers and fight for their release and rehabilitation through India's court system. Although thousands have been freed, millions more remain in slavery.

This boy was once bonded to work long hours in a carpet factory. Now he has been freed and is learning new skills.

Swami Agnivesh, of the Bonded Labor Liberation Front of India, has helped free thousands of bonded laborers.

Iqbal Masih

Iqbal Masih was bonded to work in a carpet factory by his father, to repay a loan. Iqbal won his release in 1992 after campaigners from the BLLF told him of Pakistan's new law against bonded labor. He joined their campaign and helped bring the abuses of child labor and debt bondage to international attention. Iqbal was shot and killed in April 1995 in unexplained circumstances—some claimed he had been shot by carpet-factory bosses.

Child workers

Children work all over the world. Most common is unpaid work at home or in family businesses, but children also work in paid employment. In Western countries working children are likely to be teenagers, who combine part-time work (such as paper routes or baby-sitting) with school or take paid jobs during school vacations.

Today, most children in poorer countries also attend school. However, most leave school and begin work at an earlier age than Western children. The poorest children are likely to begin their working lives when they are very young, and, if they go to school at all, they attend irregularly and drop out early. These children are also likely to work in the dirtiest and most dangerous jobs, often for the lowest wages or even no wages at all.

Worldwide, the most common forms of child work are domestic tasks (at home or as other people's servants) or in farming or family businesses. Some children work in factories, stores, coffee houses, restaurants, and hotels, for wages or as bonded laborers. In some countries children also work (and sometimes live) on the streets—running errands, carrying shopping, shining shoes, and finding and selling bottles and cardboard. Some children combine part-time work with school, and others work full-time. During busy seasons (such as plowing, planting, and harvesting) children and adults in rural areas work long hours. They then spend months without work.

In Calcutta, India, 13-year-old Anuj earns a tiny wage recycling batteries. He is at risk of being poisoned by mercury.

The great debate

Whether children should work at all, the age at which they should start work, and the type of work they should do are all controversial issues. Some campaigners believe that all child work is wrong and argue for laws to raise the working age. They point out that young children worked in the factories and mills of Europe and North America until laws were passed banning them from dangerous jobs and making education compulsory. Other campaigners argue that a ban is unrealistic, especially in poor countries where children's earnings contribute to the family income. In these circumstances, children will continue to work whatever the law says.

In Western countries, children often earn an allowance by working in the home—but they are rarely exploited.

The Rights of the Child

Despite their differences, all campaigners agree that there are some jobs and industries where children should never be employed. Article 32 of the United Nations Convention on the Rights of the Child says that children should be "protected from economic exploitation and from performing any work that is likely to be hazardous or to interfere with the child's education, or to be harmful to the child's health or physical, mental, spiritual, moral, or social development." Other international bodies, such as the International Labor Organization (ILO), and most governments have similar laws or guidelines.

Children in danger

What kind of work is dangerous and hazardous for children? It might be work for which children are too small or too young. Perhaps it is work so hard and repetitive that it damages children's growing bodies or does not develop their minds. It might be that the working hours are too long or that the children are paid too little. Often the working environment is dangerous, with high levels of noise, dust, or chemicals or the use of unprotected machinery.

Hazardous work for children includes most tasks in mining, construction, heavy agriculture, heavy industry, and the commercial sex trade. It may also include work in light industries, service industries, domestic service, work in the home, and work on the streets. It all depends on the type of work, the hours, and the payment. Children rarely choose to work in hazardous or exploitative jobs.

Boys working in the silk industry in southern India. Despite the old-fashioned machinery, this scene comes from 1991.

Case study: Fernando's story

Eleven-year-old Fernando is one of thousands of children who work in the sugar industry of the Zona da Mata in northeastern Brazil. He does not receive a wage. Any cane he cuts is counted as part of his father's quota—to enable his father to earn a basic wage. His father tries to protect Fernando from the worst work; many of the children have had accidents with heavy tools.

Fernando is a slave because he is doing work unsuitable for a child. He is working long hours in a dangerous environment. Fernando looks much younger than 11, because he has been malnourished most of his life. Like most of the other children, he cannot read or write, since he has had to miss school during the harvest season. Fernando's family are also slaves. The only work available is in the cane fields, where wages are very low and conditions very poor. The owners of the farms are powerful people who will not allow their workers to join unions and will not improve conditions. If they raised adult wages, then children would not need to work. But the farm owners' priorities are profits, not people.

Landowners also own the land on which the laborers live. If the laborers could use some of that land to grow vegetables, they could improve their diet and health. They are not allowed to do this because every bit of land is used for growing sugar. The Brazilian government encourages the export of sugar by giving financial aid to landowners. But none of these benefits filter down to the laborers. Although the Zona da Mata is a rich and fertile area, laborers can expect to live only until the age of 46—most other Brazilians live 17 years longer than that.

The real price of sugar—a child laborer risks life and health on a South American sugar plantation.

Why use child workers?

Children are especially vulnerable when employers claim that their small size and tiny fingers are an advantage. Around 750,000 children work in the carpet industry in Asia, mainly in India and Pakistan. While the most complex and expensive carpets are woven by adults, some factories making lower-quality products use child workers.

These child laborers in Thailand are imprisoned day and night to keep them from running away.

In the worst cases, in northern India and Pakistan, young children are bonded to factory owners or even kidnapped. Once in the carpet factories, children are forced to work long hours—20 hours a day has been recorded—without a break or adequate food. Most workplaces are small, poorly lit, and badly ventilated. The children suffer from stunted limbs and poor eyesight as a result. These are extreme cases, but together they add up to hundreds of thousands of child slaves.

Cheap products

Industries producing goods for export attract particular attention from organizations campaigning against child labor. Weaving carpets, sewing clothing, stitching soccer balls and baseballs—all these industries have used and abused children's labor to produce goods cheaply. Some of these industries have been pinpointed by campaigners or boycotted. Sometimes the effect of these campaigns has been to make the situation worse (see pages 58–59).

But worldwide, only about 5 percent of the child workers are in export industries. Most produce goods for their home market—food, matches, cigarettes, bricks, fireworks, locks—or they provide services such as selling, carrying, collecting, and repairing goods or cleaning and performing other domestic tasks for people.

Fishing platforms

In 1996, the bodies of two teenage boys were found washed up on a beach in Sumatra, Indonesia. The boys had been working on illegal fishing platforms five miles (8 km) off the coast. They had slipped while pulling in nets. Thousands of young boys work three-month shifts on the platforms. Some of them are kidnapped. Others are tricked into believing they will earn good money. They find themselves trapped on the platforms, doing dangerous and lonely work.

Children in India prepare matches for dipping in phosphorus—a very dangerous task.

Talking point

"From an employer's point of view, child labor is perhaps the most stable form of labor; children do not strike or disrupt production. On the other hand, they are also the easiest to dislodge in times of economic difficulty. Children are the cheapest to hire and the easiest to fire. They do not resist. They are physically and emotionally vulnerable and are often abused or threatened."

A. Bequele, *Combating Child Labour*, International Labor Organization, 1991

What are the arguments against using child labor?

What is a child?

It is virtually impossible to know how many children work on a regular basis for more than just a few hours a day. The most recent International Labor Organization estimates are that there are 250 million working children ages 5 to 14, with about 150 million in Asia, and most of the others in Africa and South America. Although many of these children work in appalling conditions that would not be acceptable in Western countries, they are not slaves —they can leave or change jobs, and their wages support themselves and their families.

It is not easy to define the difference between children and adults. The United Nations Convention on the Rights of the Child defines children as people under 18 years of age, and in most countries this is the age of public citizenship (for example, when people get the right to vote).

In practice, in many societies childhood ends much earlier, and young people can and do work, accept responsibility, marry, and have children before the age of 18.

Child marriage is illegal in India—but it continues to take place. Here a girl of 5 is married to a 15-year-old boy while their families look on.

Working for export

In India and Pakistan, stitching leather goods is a traditional industry. Some towns, such as Sialkot in Pakistan, stitch soccer balls, which are sold for high prices in Western countries. Local and international organizations pointed out that some small children were working alongside adults. They campaigned to end child labor in the industry, and placed pressure on companies to increase adult wages so that children could attend school. Campaigns against this and similar situations continue.

Many countries have been shocked to see young children working long hours in factories and farms, and this has prompted many campaigns by local and international organizations to raise the working age and to improve conditions.

Child workers in rich countries

Most hazardous child labor takes place in poor countries. However, cases can be found in rich countries. Children work in shoemaking in Portugal and Italy and in clothing factories and farming in the United States. A 1990 survey of Mexican-American children working on farms in New York State revealed that almost half worked in fields still wet with pesticides; of that, a third had been sprayed with pesticides while working.

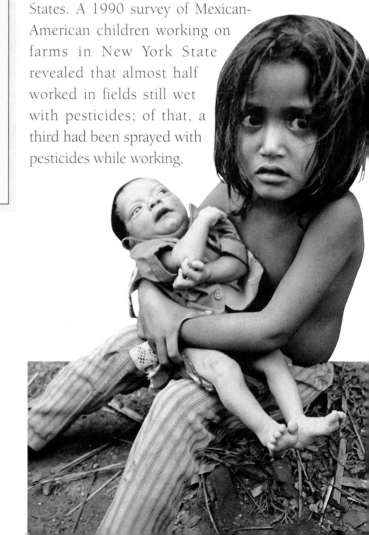

A common scene from Bangladesh. Girls often stay at home and miss school to care for younger children.

Child domestic servants

In most households children are expected to do some housework. In Western countries this is usually "helping out" around the home. There is often a "wage" in the form of pocket money or allowances. However much children may dislike these jobs, most could not say that they are tough or unfair.

Child domestic servants

In many countries it is common for children to work as domestic servants in the homes of other people— often complete strangers living far away. These children—most of whom are girls—are not "helping out," but are doing full-time jobs.

In poor countries, running water or electricity may be infrequently available or nonexistent, and there are few labor-saving devices like vacuum cleaners or washing machines. The main burden of housework is carried by servants. In many households, the youngest and most put-upon servant is usually a girl domestic. Most of these girls are under the age of 14, and some are only five or six.

In Africa it is common for many girls to work in other people's households. This young servant works in Dakar, capital of Senegal.

Talking point

"Child domestic workers are the world's most forgotten children. Although domestic service need not be hazardous, it is often just that. Children in domestic service may well be the most vulnerable and exploited children of all, as well as the most difficult to protect."

UNICEF *State of the World's Children*, 1997

Can you think of ways to keep young children from becoming domestic servants?

For a few girls, the experience of domestic work is a positive one. They learn new skills and are treated as members of the family. Some girls from poor farming families are sent to relatives to better themselves. In parts of Africa it is traditional for a girl to work in a relative's household.

But a girl is more likely to find domestic service an exploitative and isolating experience. The chances are that she will work long hours for little or no pay, she will not be able to go to school or learn useful skills, and she will see little of the outside world. She may also be badly treated, beaten, or even may be sexually abused.

Haiti's "restaveks"

Like many other child domestic workers, the "restaveks" of Haiti, in the Caribbean, come from poor, rural families. They are taken by their "employers" to the city and lose all contact with their families. Their employer can pass them on to another family or throw them on the street for the smallest mistake. Some run away. Many of the children living in the streets of Port-au-Prince, the capital, are former domestic servants. Although street life is hard, they prefer it to domestic slavery.

In 1996 shocked neighbors in Kathmandu, Nepal, told police how Dhirj, a 12-year-old servant, was chained and imprisoned. His master was arrested.

31

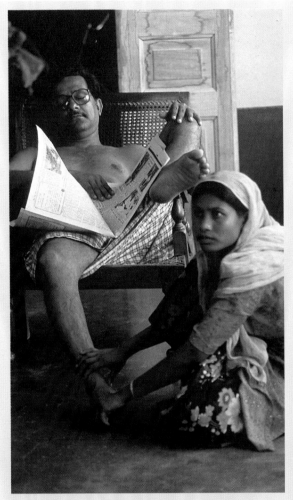

Most domestic servants in Bangladesh are expected to be on call at all hours. This girl is massaging her employer's feet.

Case study: Hassina's story

Sheela from India, whom we met on pages 8 and 9, is one of millions of girl domestics worldwide. Hassina, a 10-year-old from Dhaka, the capital of Bangladesh, is another. Unlike Sheela, who comes from a small village, Hassina has always lived in the city, and she has always been a servant. Hassina is a *bandua*, the local term for a full-time, live-in servant. Hassina was regarded as an extra mouth to feed by her family. When she was seven, one family offered to employ her on a permanent basis as a *bandua*. Hassina's family was given some money in advance and told they would receive more as Hassina became older and more experienced.

Hassina found her new life bewildering, separated from her family and plunged into a different world. Hassina's main task was looking after a toddler. But she was also expected to do other work, such as helping out in the kitchen and running errands. When she was nine, Hassina went to live as a *bandua* with another family on the other side of Dhaka. She no longer saw her mother regularly, and there was no easy way to keep in touch—neither she nor her mother can read or write and she could not afford to phone.

Hassina begins work before the other household members are awake. She is responsible for waking, bathing, dressing, and feeding the family's children, even though they are only a few years younger than she is. She walks them to and from school. In the hours in between she works in the house—sweeping and mopping floors and washing clothes. She helps out in the kitchen. She serves the evening meal and removes and washes the dishes. In the evening, when the family members relax, she is still on call. If unexpected guests arrive or the children are sick, she will be expected to provide food and care.

Hassina does not have a work contract outlining her tasks or hours of work. Nor does she receive wages. Her family does receive some money, but she never sees it. In return for her work she receives food, clothing, and shelter. Her food is mainly leftovers, and she eats alone in the kitchen. Sometimes her employer gives her cast-off clothing. She shares a room with the family children, but while they sleep on comfortable beds, she sleeps on a mat on the floor.

Many domestic workers have endless chores and never even get to leave the house in which they work.

Hassina's employer feels that she treats Hassina well. After all, she feeds her, looks after her, and does not give her many hard duties. Nor does she beat or abuse her like many other employers. She thinks Hassina should be grateful for being her *bandua*. Hassina's family is also content. The family says that she is helping to support them while being removed from the dangers of street life.

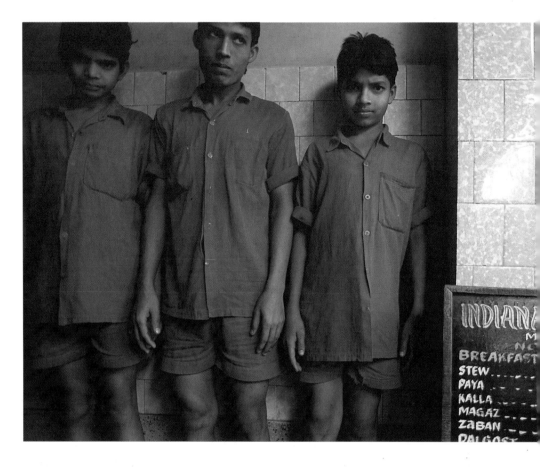

A common sight in India—young boys waiting on tables and working in restaurant kitchens

Learning to live with slavery

Hassina, and those like her, may be considered slaves in that they have been sent away from home, have no control over their work or leisure time, and they are not paid for their work. Some children also do hazardous work for long hours. Compared with some child servants, Hassina is not badly treated—she is not abused physically or sexually, and she is not locked in the house. If she were very brave, she could probably leave her employer, but there are few other opportunities—she would probably end up as a *bandua* somewhere else or on the streets. When she is older, she may be able to leave. In the meantime, she has learned to obey her employer and not complain.

There are no real figures on the number of children working as domestic servants, although they must total millions. Child servants are common in southern Asia and in many countries in Southeast Asia, Africa, and South and Central America. Although not all child servants are slaves, the conditions of work and the isolation of the child give no protection against exploitation.

What is in a name?
The local words for child servants reveal how society sees them. These include *bandua* (tied-down) in Bangladesh, *puerta cerada* (closed door) in the Dominican Republic, and *restaveks* (from "rester avec"—to stay with) in Haiti.

These children are no longer slaves, but their future remains uncertain. To rebuild their lives, they need homes, families, education, and income.

Waiting on customers
Some children work in coffee shops, cafés, restaurants, hotels, and rooming houses. Hours are long, and work can be dangerous. Customers, bosses, or older workers may be demanding or violent. Children may sleep in corridors, on tables, or even outside. However, this type of work is generally less isolating than household service, and there are more opportunities to learn skills.

Trafficking in people

Leaving home

"I did not know where I was going. I hoped that it would not be too far from home. But going to another country is much worse. Here, everyone is a stranger. I cannot speak their language. All I do is work all day. I want to go home." (Marie, age 11, Togo)

Marie is part of the worldwide traffic in young people. Trafficking is the business of taking people from their community by force or by deceit. The victims find themselves trapped in situations from which they cannot escape. Trafficking in people is a profitable business, although no one knows how profitable. It is also an unlawful and secretive business. It is often dangerous. On Christmas Day 1996, 250 would-be migrants from southern Asia drowned in the Mediterranean Sea when their boat capsized. Each one had paid high prices to the traffickers.

Most young girls in Togo are expected to do domestic tasks. Today, increasing numbers are trafficked to the oil-rich countries of Nigeria and Gabon.

West Africa

Trafficking in children is a growing problem in West Africa—the countries involved include Benin, Togo, Nigeria, Niger, Burkina Faso, and Gabon. Eleven-year-old Marie is one of thousands of girls from rural Togo working as domestic servants in the oil-rich countries of Nigeria and Gabon. As the eldest girl in a large family, she was sent to work for a family in Lomé, the largest settlement in Togo.

Her parents trusted the agent, who promised them that Marie would improve her domestic skills, while sending money home to help educate her brothers. What neither they nor Marie knew was that Marie would be sent to another country.

The agent first took Marie to Lomé. Then she was smuggled across international borders and kept with other girls in a locked building in a large city— she does not know where. One day, the girls were taken to the docks and put on a ship. The journey was frightening; the ship was unseaworthy and many girls were sick.

When the ship docked in Gabon, the girls were separated and sent to work as servants. A few were well treated and were even able to send money back home. But most were like Marie, forced to work for long hours, without pay and with hardly any food. If her "employers" disliked her work, she was beaten.

Selling vegetables in the street brings only a small income, but it is not as dangerous or exploitative as working as a domestic servant far from home.

Stop the child traffickers

In 1993 a Togolese diplomat in Gabon urged his government to stop the traffic in children. He wrote: "The conditions in which these children are working here is inhuman. Those employed as domestic servants suffer terrible ill-treatment ... the Gabonese do not hesitate to call it slavery." A local campaigning organization, WAO Afrique, also urged government action. But as long as families are poor and girls are less valued than boys, greedy and unscrupulous people will be prepared to continue the traffic.

Prostitution is always slavery when children are involved. These young girls work at a brothel in Cambodia.

Case study: Thaldee's story

"I thought that I'd be working in a factory, not in a brothel. I do not like it here, we have to work every day and there are lots of men. I must make a lot of money for the owner, but I do not see it. At least if I could send money home, I'd feel that it was worthwhile." (Thaldee, Thailand)

In the northeast of Thailand, where Thaldee lives, girls are less valued than boys. When her parents told her that she would be working far away, Thaldee obeyed her family. Thaldee was taken to her new workplace—a brothel. Once there, she was kept in a locked room. From then on, each night men would arrive and pay money to be with her. Thaldee was 14 at the time. Some girls in the brothel were older, but others were much younger.

Since then Thaldee has been working long hours. She has no say over how many men she must serve or the conditions in which she works. None of the clients' money goes to Thaldee—all she gets is food and some clothing. She is sometimes beaten, either by the client or the brothel owner.

After a year, Thaldee was sold to a larger brothel where the clients paid higher rates. The owner told Thaldee that if she wanted to leave she must first pay off her debt and then repay all the money he had spent on her food and clothing.

Thaldee has learned how to cope with difficult situations and how to earn tips from clients. She keeps this extra money secret from the owner. The girls are sometimes allowed out during the day, so they could probably escape—but Thaldee wants to return home with money, so she stays where she is.

Thaldee worries about her family. In fact, her family may have known she would be working in a brothel. Although the Thai government and local campaigning groups warn families about the dangers of trafficking and the sex industry, the trade continues because the financial rewards can be high.

Similar stories could be told in many countries. Trafficking takes place within countries and across borders, especially across land borders.

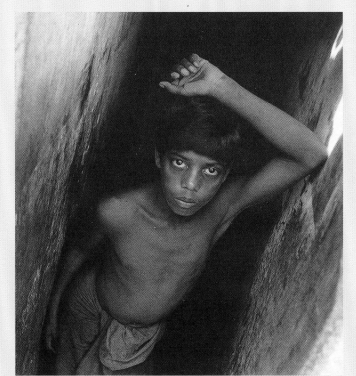

In some countries boys also become enslaved in the sex industry. This young prostitute is from Sri Lanka.

Is prostitution slavery?

Prostitution—the selling of sexual services—is a difficult and controversial issue. Some people believe that all paid sex, even between consenting adults, is wrong and exploitative. The opposite view is that selling sex is like any other job and, therefore, should be made legal and safe. However, both sides agree that prostitution is slavery when it involves children and young people (because the work is hazardous, and they cannot give legal consent). It is also considered slavery when people (whatever their age) are sold, forced, or tricked into working in the sex industry and are not free to leave.

Some campaigning organizations estimate that up to one million girls today have been forced or tricked into the sex industry through trafficking. Like other slaves, they find escape almost impossible. Sometimes they are locked up during the day and closely supervised while they are working. If they are in a foreign country, they may not speak the language, which makes them especially helpless and isolated. If they manage to pay off their debts and return to their homes, they may find they face discrimination from their families and community or find it difficult to marry. As a result, many remain at work in the sex industry.

In some countries, such as India, the children of prostitutes face discrimination. For example, most do not have a family name and are not allowed to attend school. Without schooling or opportunities, they are likely to follow their mothers into prostitution.

Prostitutes like these women in Mumbai continue working to pay off debts. Society discriminates against them and their children.

Talking point

"Sexual slavery is a meaningless idea. Slavery involving sexual services, carpet weaving, or any other form of labor is so abhorrent that it is pointless to qualify it. What are these people saying? That one form of slavery is worse than another or should be abolished sooner? Slavery is slavery is slavery."

Network of Sex Worker Projects, Bulletin, June 1995

Are some forms of slavery worse than others?

Child camel jockeys

Other victims of trafficking include boys who are forced to work as camel jockeys. Trafficked boys serve as jockeys in the United Arab Emirates (UAE) in the Middle East. The boys, often only four or five years old, come from very poor families in Pakistan, India, Bangladesh, Sudan, Eritrea, and Mauritania. They are either kidnapped, sold by their families, or taken by deceit.

Camel races are frantic and dangerous. The screaming boys are strapped to the camels and are often injured. Some are even killed. Stranded in a strange country, the boys are often mistreated and abused. Although the use of child jockeys in UAE was banned in 1993, it continues to take place.

Racing for their lives. Children continue to act as camel jockeys, even though the practice is officially banned in the United Arab Emirates.

Migrant workers

International migration is part of modern life. People move from one country to another, mainly from poor to richer countries, sometimes to settle permanently, but mainly to work. One estimate is that there are 50 million migrant workers worldwide, including 30 million illegal workers (without immigration papers). While most migration is within a country, some migration is international. Some migrants are recruited into good jobs, but most do the jobs local people do not want—jobs that are hazardous, with the lowest pay and status.

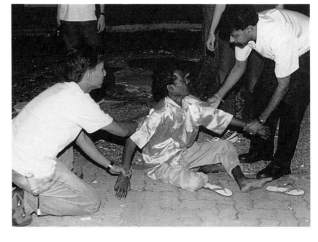

If immigrant workers are found to be working illegally, they may be arrested and deported.

Migrants: illegal and legal

Some migrants travel legally—they enter a country with the government's approval. Others are illegal migrants who come into a country without permission. Because they are in a country illegally, these migrants live in an in-between world. They are afraid of complaining against bad treatment for fear that they will be found out and sent home. They cannot use social services, such as health care, because they do not exist in law. This leaves them especially vulnerable to exploitation.

Most migrants have chosen to move in order to earn money and improve their lives. Although many experience difficulties, they are not slaves. They can change their employers, their workplace, or the work they do, even though their choices may be limited. But some migrant workers do not have even these opportunities. They are slaves.

Domestic servitude

Some of the worst abuses occur where migrants work as domestic servants. Like child domestic workers, they are often confined in their employers' houses and isolated from people who might be able to help them. If they are cheated of their wages or abused by their employers, they have no one to turn to. As foreigners, they may not understand the local language or culture.

Many migrant domestic workers are found in the oil-rich countries of the Middle East—Saudi Arabia, Kuwait, and the United Arab Emirates. Almost all domestic workers are women. Around half come from Sri Lanka, while others come from the Philippines, India, and Indonesia. Most are recruited by agencies in their countries, who charge them a high fee for finding them a job and for the airfare. The worker must repay the costs from her new job. Many women are unskilled. Others, especially from the Philippines, are well educated but cannot find good jobs in their own country. Many leave their children, hoping to make enough money during their time overseas to repay their debts and assist their families.

Exploitation

Illegal immigrants are at particular risk of abuse and exploitation. Every year thousands of Mexican workers are smuggled into the United States. Most work in agricultural jobs—picking fruit and vegetables, unprotected from hazardous pesticides. They are not only paid lower than minimum wages and housed in poor conditions, but also may be threatened with violence if they protest. In other cases, Mexican immigrants have been promised jobs as domestics but are forced into prostitution.

Rich countries try to stop illegal migrants from entering their borders by putting up barbed wire and electric fences, but desperation drives people on.

Trapped and abused

In the Middle East, domestic workers often work long hours without a break. They are frequently mistreated and are sometimes abused and raped. The contract of employment forbids the worker to take other jobs, and she cannot return home until she has repaid her debts. In any case, she cannot travel because her employer has her passport.

Unfair contracts

Even a written contract is no guarantee of fair treatment. In 1990 a typical contract for domestic workers in the Middle East stated: "Her duty hours will be unlimited as she will be treated as one of the family household. She will not be allowed out of the house alone. There is no holiday for housemaids.... She must not refuse any duties given to her." This contract places a worker in a situation similar to slavery. It is easy to imagine that such a situation occurs only in the Middle East. But it also takes place in many Western countries.

There are thousands of foreign domestic workers in Great Britain. They are the servants of foreign diplomats, businessmen, and visitors and of British people returning from working abroad. For 18 years, between 1980 and 1998, the government allowed rich visitors to bring domestic servants to Great Britain. The domestics were regarded as members of their employer's household, not as individuals. Although British law gives workers various rights, some of these did not apply to foreign domestic workers. If they were abused by their employer or wanted to improve their conditions, they could not change jobs.

Not all domestic work is exploitative. Many people throughout the world work for fair employers.

Talking point

"There is no doubt that slavery is taking place in England. Who would have thought that such a state was possible?"

The Earl of Longford, describing conditions of foreign domestic workers, November 1990

Does slavery exist in your country? If it does, how do you think it could be ended?

One human rights organization in the UK that campaigns for overseas domestic servants is Kalayaan. It has more than 2,000 cases of people who have run away from their employers. They tell of being imprisoned, beaten, and raped. Because many of the workers cannot speak English very well, they are doubly imprisoned; first by their employers and second by isolation.

Women migrant workers and supporters of Kalayaan meet to promote the fight for improved working conditions.

Thousands of women from the Philippines work as domestic servants in Great Britain. They often have to leave their families behind them.

Case study: Erlinda's tale

Erlinda used to think of herself as a slave. Now she is a TNT—*Tago ng tago*. In Erlinda's "Tagalog" language, this phrase means "hide and hide." Erlinda is from the Philippines and started work as a domestic servant in Dubai, in the United Arab Emirates. She was badly treated there, but her life became much worse when her employer brought her to London.

In Dubai the family had several servants, but in London Erlinda was alone. Not only was she expected to do all the work, but she also became the target of all the abuse of which the family was capable. She had to be available at any time for any family member—even the tiny children. When she was allowed to sleep, it was on the floor of a cold corridor. She ate leftovers from the meals she had cooked. She was constantly called names—dog, pig, slave —and was regularly beaten. She could not leave the house, not even to go to church on Sundays.

Finally, Erlinda could stand it no longer and escaped, with the help of a neighbor. She was alone in a strange city, without money, without papers or even her passport. Finally, she met another Filipina who took her to a center that helped abused domestic workers. Here she met other women in her position. The center helped find her a place to stay and advised her on what she should do. They also helped her take action against her former employer and to get her passport and unpaid wages from her employer. But all this took a long time.

Erlinda had hoped to find another domestic job and earn money to repay her debts and send to her family in the Philippines. But she was not allowed to do this legally. Although she did eventually find work, it was poorly paid, but she could not complain, because she was working illegally. She felt that she could not register with a doctor or open a bank account, for she had by now overstayed her original visa. She is terrified of being found and deported. She is no longer a slave, but as a TNT she is still imprisoned by her situation.

Three Filipinas prepare to speak out against modern slavery in Great Britain in 1995. They are visiting the memorial to the 1833 Law to Abolish Slavery in the British colonies.

Forced labor

We have seen that there are many types of slavery. But they all involve individuals, families, or companies, enslaving other people. It is natural to expect governments to take action against cases of slavery. But what happens when it is the government that acts as the slave master?

During the twentieth century, millions of people have become the prisoners of dictatorships that crush any opposition and control people's lives. The former Soviet Union put millions of political prisoners into slave labor camps. Similarly, Germany under the National Socialists (Nazis) used prisoners and concentration-camp inmates as slave labor. In the People's Republic of China, millions of prisoners spend years in slave labor camps.

Forced labor by governments

One country that still enslaves its own people is Burma, which has been ruled by a military dictatorship since 1962. Repression has continued ever since, despite international criticism of the government's actions.

The military dictatorship in Burma, in power since 1962, is prepared to use the force of soldiers against those who protest for democracy.

Jiangbei Prison, in Hubei province, is one of China's largest prison camps, with more than 10,000 prisoners.

How big is the problem?

It is very hard to estimate how many people are involved in forced labor across the world. Governments usually deny that it exists, journalists are forbidden to investigate, and labor camps are often situated in remote areas. In Burma the number of forced laborers must run into hundreds of thousands (perhaps millions), while Asia Watch (a human rights group) estimates that there are over one million prisoners in labor reform camps in China.

One of the worst aspects of life in Burma is that the government forces people to work for it without pay and in terrible conditions. The army, known as *tatmadaw*, dominates people's lives. It has forced thousands of people to become porters, carrying heavy loads. Porters must provide their own food and are unpaid. They are beaten, raped, tortured, or killed while trying to escape. Others have died from illness or exhaustion.

Tradition or slavery?

Burma's government wanted to improve communications and transportation. It also hoped to make Burma more attractive for foreign businesses and tourists. But the cost of the improvements was high, and the country was almost bankrupt. In 1990, the government ordered the people of Burma to work without payment.

The Burmese government tries to justify this by saying that people are following a traditional practice called *loke a pei*—voluntary work for the benefit of the community. But, in fact, what is happening is neither voluntary nor traditional. It is forced labor, carried out on such a scale and with such brutality that it can only be described as slavery.

Forced labor system

This is how the system works in Burma. When labor is needed, the local army commander delivers a signed order to each village head. The letter says bluntly: "Send [number] voluntary workers from [name] village to [name of army camp] on [date] without fail. One of the village leaders must come with the group. Bring along a list of villagers who fail to come." If the village head does not obey the order, villagers are severely punished. Villagers must supply their own food and tools. If the work site is far from the village, people must sleep there without food, water, or shelter.

Under this system, hundreds of thousands of people have been forced to work against their will and without payment. They build airports, roads, dams, railroad lines, and power plants. Some parents send children to serve in their place. Labor can continue for days, weeks, or months. Farms and businesses are neglected and abandoned, so harvests fail and local economies suffer. As a result the community as a whole suffers, and many people have fled to neighboring countries or areas outside government control.

The heavy chains limit movement, but this Burmese prisoner is still expected to undertake hard labor all day without payment.

Tourism: what is the cost?

1996 was to be "Visit Myanmar Year" (Myanmar is the new name the government has chosen for Burma). This meant building more hotels and more roads and improving the historic sites. Part of the preparation for the tourist year was to "clean up" Mandalay Palace in the city center. This meant widening roads and dredging the palace moat. This gigantic task was carried out by 2,000 conscripted laborers. Some of the workers were prisoners. Others were city people and farmers.

Visit Myanmar Year was not a success. Those tourists who did go to Burma were no help to the local people—over half the profits went to foreign investors, and most of the remainder went to the government.

Talking point

"Murder is traditional, rape is traditional, torture is traditional. It is all traditional—but it does not make it right. If any of this abuse was traditional practice, there would not be thousands of refugees on Burma's borders. If it was a traditional and acceptable practice, people would not be fleeing it.... Forced labor is slavery."

Representative of the Australia-Burma Council, giving evidence to the Australian Parliament, May 1995

Are human rights violations such as slavery ever acceptable?

The glittering lights of Mandalay Palace reflected in the moat. All the restoration work on the palace was done with forced labor.

Case study: Harry Wu's story

In 1960, Communist party authorities in China arrested Harry Wu as a "counterrevolutionary." For ten years he was sent from one prison camp to another. He was confined, beaten, and forced to work in dreadful conditions. Later he had to work in a coal mine in a remote area. He was finally released after 19 years of forced labor.

Finally, he was allowed to emigrate to the United States. He twice returned secretly to China to investigate conditions in labor camps and prisons—at great risk to himself. His aim was to tell people about the use of forced labor in Chinese labor "reform" camps making goods for export. He was arrested on one trip to China in 1998, but eventually released after friends, family, journalists, politicians, and human rights organizations put a lot of pressure on the Chinese government.

Harry Wu talks of his experiences openly. "The experience of 19 years in the camps kept streaming back into my mind.... How could I turn my back on what I had witnessed? .... Returning to China holds great dangers for me, not the least of which is the possibility of once more losing the freedom and happiness that were so hard to come by in the first place and of causing my beloved wife to endure a lifetime of sadness and pain."

Hard manual labor remains a way of life in China's prisons, today as in the 1960s when this photo was taken.

Comfort women in Korea

Forced labor takes many forms. The story of the "comfort women" of Korea dates back to World War II. Lee Sun-dok was one of thousands of Korean "comfort women" enslaved by the Japanese Army during the 1930s. In 1937 she was confined in a military brothel and forced to provide sex for Japanese soldiers. Her imprisonment lasted until World War II ended in 1945. Lee Sun-dok and other women spent years fighting for compensation and an apology from the Japanese government. In 1998 a Japanese court said that her human rights had been violated. Mrs. Lee said that the small compensation she received (the equivalent of $2,000) was an insult to the women, "who were treated lower than human beings."

Although they are old and frail, Korean women who were enslaved by the Japanese Army continue their fight for justice.

Breaking the chains

Talking point

"Our fellow young workers who were terminated from the garment industry have either become child prostitutes or brick breakers or garbage collectors ... we appeal to allow us to continue our light work for 5–6 hours a day and give us an opportunity to attend school for 2–3 hours a day. If you find child workers in any hazardous or heavy work, bring them back to light work. Do not throw away on the street those of us who are already involved in some kind of light work."

Petition from child workers, Bangladesh, 1994

Do you think it is ever right for children to work for a living?

Slavery is based on violence and intimidation. This woman in Burma has been ordered to work by the military.

This book features some of the most common forms of modern slavery—traditional slavery, debt bondage, hazardous child labor, forced domestic service, trafficking in people, exploitative migrant labor, and forced labor by governments. But whatever the label, slavery cannot be justified.

The Atlantic slave trade was promoted by greed for financial gain, and slavery remains a profitable business today. However, it is no longer seen as something lawful and respectable, but as illegal and shameful. Those who benefit from slavery either deny that it exists at all or say that it benefits both sides. Yet, if slavery is so beneficial, why is it based on the use of violence and intimidation?

Effective government laws, backed by international standards, must aim to improve the lives of working children.

What is the solution?

How can we end slavery? There are no easy answers to this question. As we have seen, slavery takes many forms. Each will demand a different response. Nevertheless, we can learn lessons from past and present experiences of ending slavery.

Human rights

Slavery is a violation of people's most basic human rights—the right to control their own bodies, to use and enjoy the rewards of their labor, and to make and act on their own decisions. These basic rights are summed up by Article 3 of the Universal Declaration of Human Rights: "Everyone has the right to life, liberty, and security of person." Slavery violates these rights because it deprives people of life, liberty, and security.

Slaves cannot escape their plight alone. It is very difficult for slaves to gain their freedom without outside support. Slaves are "tied"—to a master, to a place, or to a debt. Many are young children, locked in factories or in their masters' houses. If they try to escape they may be captured and beaten, or even killed. Those who escape are unlikely to have the skills and the contacts to find a place to live or get a good job or even to know their basic rights as citizens. Their physical and emotional health may be affected by years of hard labor, imprisonment, and abuse. In any case, even if some slaves escape, others may take their place.

Public pressure

Public pressure and campaigning are vital. Slaves need support and assistance from individuals and from non-governmental organizations (NGOs). Some of the most effective NGOs are local organizations of former slaves, like SOS Esclaves in Mauritania. They know the conditions and experiences of slaves and the best ways to support them.

Government action is also necessary. Governments must recognize slavery and take action against it. This means ending trafficking in people, releasing and rehabilitating enslaved people, and punishing all those involved in promoting slavery.

Rugmark

How can people ensure that goods, such as handwoven carpets, are not made by exploited children? After campaigns in South Asia, by local and international NGOs, some companies have agreed to independent inspection of carpet factories and have drawn up guidelines or codes of conduct for their suppliers to follow. Carpets produced without child exploitation can then carry a special "rugmark" label to guide consumers.

More children in class means fewer children working in exploitative conditions. This school is in India, where more children now attend elementary school than ever before.

Probably the most difficult task is assisting former slaves to become independent. For example, a young child might need education, whereas a teenager or adult may prefer work retraining or a business loan. Land reform is also important—former bonded laborers need land to support their families. Former slaves may need health or welfare services or legal advice. However, poor countries may lack the resources to carry out these programs.

International action

International action takes careful thought. The United Nations and its agencies have developed human rights conventions and international labor standards. Although most governments agree to these standards, they are often ignored or not put in place. Many campaigners face indifference or hostility from governments and people who profit from slavery.

One of the most important tasks facing NGOs is to ensure that governments and international agencies have accurate information. Slavery is an emotional subject and it is easy to get the facts wrong—leading to responses that may make the situation worse.

Listening to the experts

In 1975 the United Nations Human Rights Commission established the UN Working Group on Contemporary Forms of Slavery. Each year a group of experts meets in Geneva and listens to evidence from NGOs about slavery. The group asks governments to say what action they are taking to end slavery and makes recommendations to governments and UN agencies to support anti-slavery initiatives.

The United Nations in Geneva is a focal point for international action against slavery.

The final stage of the Global March Against Child Labor reaches the International Labor Organization in Geneva, June 1998.

Global March

From January to June 1998 a Global March Against Child Labor drew international attention to the conditions faced by the world's 250 million working children. The march was organized by campaigning organizations and featured young workers from five continents. The march finished at the UN in Geneva, where it lobbied the International Labor Organization to improve conditions for working children. The ILO hopes to mark the new millennium by agreeing on a new International Convention banning the most hazardous forms of child labor. If agreed to and accepted by governments, the Convention will be a big step forward for the human rights of working children.

Media pressure

Foreign governments sometimes become involved in taking action against slavery in other countries, mainly in response to public campaigns or media reports. This can be helpful when governments take care to understand the situation and to give extra resources to poor countries. However, international action can also be harmful.

One example concerns the use of child labor. In 1992 the U.S. Congress proposed to ban imports to the United States of products made using workers under 15 years of age. The country most affected was Bangladesh, where clothing factories employed young women workers, some of whom were under 15. Factories began to fire young workers, who lost the income needed to support their families. As a result, young workers had to find new jobs—normally in much worse and more hazardous conditions. Rather than helping children escape slavery, the proposed measure pushed many into slavery. It was later agreed that older children could continue factory work. International support was given to new projects to provide schooling and job training, often on a part-time basis, to younger children.

This one example shows how complex the issues are and how difficult it can be to find workable solutions. Slavery is not a single issue, but part of the poverty and violence that affects the lives of millions of people. Ending slavery will take much more than fine words and good laws. It will need understanding and determination, together with resources and support, to ensure that the chains of slavery are completely broken.

Happy children at play in Nepal—even the poorest countries can work toward ending slavery.

Glossary

Atlantic slave trade The trafficking in Africans by European slave traders, mainly for sale to European plantation owners in the Americas, continuing over four centuries (1450 to 1870).

Bonded labor A term used for debt bondage in southern Asia (India, Pakistan, and Nepal).

Boycott Refusal to buy certain goods, for example, those made by children.

Brothel A place where paid sex takes place.

Castes Different groups or classes, some with high status and some with low status, into which people in some Asian societies are divided. People are born into a caste and cannot change from a low caste to a high caste or vice versa.

Chattel slavery Slavery that involves buying and selling people as if they were property.

Child labor Work done by children, especially young children.

Communist party The political party that ruled the former Soviet Union, and still rules the People's Republic of China and some other countries, as a dictatorship.

Contract A written or verbal agreement that is legally binding.

Debt bondage A type of slavery in which people work for others to pay off a debt and in which conditions are very exploitative.

Deported Sent out of country, banished.

Diplomat A person who represents his or her country abroad, an ambassador.

Domestic service The work performed by servants in a household.

Exploiting Working people very hard, and paying them very little (or nothing), so as to make large profits for oneself.

Filipina A woman or girl from the Philippines.

Heavy industries Industries such as steelmaking, car manufacture, mining.

Light industries Industries such as textiles, clothing, electronics.

Migrating Moving from one's home to another area or country, generally to find work.

Passport A document needed when traveling outside one's own country.

Pesticides Chemicals, used frequently in commercial farming to kill insects, etc., and sometimes hazardous to people and the environment.

Plantation A large farm growing (usually) one crop for sale, worked by laborers. In the past, many plantations were worked by slave labor.

Political prisoners People imprisoned for their political beliefs or actions.

Prostitution The selling of sex for money.

Trafficking (in human beings)
Removing people by force or deceit from their community, imprisoning them, and (sometimes) selling them, often in another country.

United Nations An international organization linking, and working for, all countries of the world.

United Nations Universal Declaration of Human Rights The basic document on human rights, accepted in 1948, and since signed by all the governments of the world.

Visa A document in a passport, needed to enter a country legally.

Books to read

Slavery in history

Douglass, Frederick. *Narrative of the Life of Frederick Douglass*. Mineola, NY: Dover Publications, Inc., 1995.

Hatt, Christine. *Slavery: from Africa to the Americas* (History in Writing). New York: Peter Bedrick Books, 1997.
Original documents on the Atlantic slave trade.

Paulsen, Gary. *Nightjohn and Sarney: A Life Remembered*. New York: Delacorte Press, 1998.
A novel on slavery in the United States.

Solzhenitsyn, Alexander. *One Day in the Life of Ivan Denisovich*. New York: Penguin, 1963.
A novel about slave labor in Siberia.

Vassilieva, Tatiana. *A Hostage to War*. New York: Scholastic Trade, 1997.
Firsthand account of slavery in Nazi Germany.

Modern slavery

Ennew, Judith. *The Exploitation of Children* (Global Issues). Austin, TX: Raintree Steck-Vaughn, 1996.
A global focus on child labor.

Gates, Doris. *Blue Willow*. New York: Viking, 1976.
A novel about a young girl's migrant-worker family in the dustbowl.

Green, Duncan. *Hidden Lives: Voices of Children in Latin America and the Caribbean*. New York: Cassell, 1998.
Young workers speak out about their lives.

Steinbeck, John. *The Grapes of Wrath*. New York: Penguin, 1992.

Turner, Mary (ed.) *From Chattel Slaves to Wage Slaves: The Dynamics of Labor Bargaining in the Americas*. Bloomington, IN: Indiana University Press, 1995.

Wu, Harry and Carolyn Wakeman. *Bitter Winds: A Memoir of my Years in China's Gulag*. New York: John Wiley and Sons, 1995.
A personal account of China's slave labor camps.

Useful addresses

Australia
Australian Anti-Slavery Society
c/o Paul Bravender Coyle
GPO Box 438c,
Melbourne, Victoria, 3001

Australian Committee for UNICEF
55 Clarence Street, Suite 903,
Sydney, NSW 2000

Canada
Beyond Borders
506 South Drive
Winnipeg, Manitoba, R3T 0B1

Canadian Anti-Slavery Society
c/o Kathleen Ruff,
561 Ballantrae Road,
West Vancouver, British Columbia

Canadian Coalition for the
Rights of Children
180 Argyle Avenue, Suite 322,
Ottawa, Ontario, K2P 1B7

Ireland
Irish National Committee for UNICEF
4 St Andrew Street,
Dublin 2

New Zealand
New Zealand Committee for UNICEF
Level 4, Wilbank Court,
57 Willis Street,
Wellington

UK
Anti-Slavery International (ASI)
Thomas Clarkson House,
The Stableyard,
Broomgrove Road,
London, SW9 9TL

Burma Action Group
Bickerton House,
25–27 Bickerton Road,
London, N19 5JT

International Save the Children
Alliance
275–281 King Street,
London, W6 9LZ

Kalayaan
St Francis of Assisi,
Pottery Lane,
London, W11 4NQ

UK Committee for UNICEF
55 Lincoln's Inn Fields,
London, WC2A 3NB

United States
Child Labor Coalition
c/o National Consumers League
1701 K Street, NW, Suite 1200,
Washington DC 200006

Human Rights Watch
350 Fifth Ave., 34th Floor,
New York, NY 10018

Index

Numbers in **bold** refer to illustrations.